Brutalist London

Owen Hopkins
Nigel Green

Blue Crow Media

Introduction

London is the antithesis of a Modernist city. Composed of myriad layers of history – and architecture – proceeding vertically and horizontally, it exists as a place of multiplicity, one that negates the very possibility of a single overarching vision, whether formal or ideological. It is partly for this reason that Modern architecture only belatedly and incompletely took hold in London, certainly before the Second World War and to some extent after, too. European Modernist architects who had fled Nazism mostly headed to the greater freedom and opportunities of the USA. So it is with some irony that it was in London that Brutalism – the most radical and bloody-minded form of Modernism – was conceived and where some of its greatest manifestations would emerge.

While Brutalism is arguably the only truly global architectural movement – and we will address this characteristic further later – the 'New Brutalism', as it was christened, was a peculiarly English, even London thing. Deriving from the French *béton brut* (raw concrete), and in that illustrating its debt to Le Corbusier, the term was popularised by the critic Reyner Banham in a widely read essay published in 1955 in the *Architectural Review*. As ever, this was the case of a critic putting a name to – and positing a theory for – a tendency that was already established, especially in the work of the Independent Group.

Chaired initially by Banham himself, the Independent Group was a loose affiliation of artists, photographers, sculptors, writers, critics – and architects – who had come together in opposition to prevailing Modernist orthodoxy. At the core of their work was an interest in mass culture, a curiosity in 'found objects' (i.e. everyday objects that could become or might be considered art) and an underlying mission to dissolve the distinction between art and life. This fascination was frequently expressed in a collagist approach, often seen as a precursor to Pop Art, which was vividly demonstrated in two influential exhibitions, *Parallel of Art and Life* at the ICA in 1953 and *This is Tomorrow* at the Whitechapel Art Gallery in 1956.

In the latter exhibition, it was the work of Eduardo Paolozzi, Nigel Henderson, Magda Cordell and especially Richard Hamilton that drew most attention, yet also notable were the contributions of architects who would soon become synonymous with Brutalism: James Stirling, Colin St John Wilson, Ernő Goldfinger and the husband-and-wife duo Alison and Peter Smithson, whose work was, for Banham, the clearest expression of the proto-movement's combination of 'ethic' and 'aesthetic', to cite his famous dichotomy.

The Smithsons were originally from the north-east of England and had met while studying in Newcastle. But they came to prominence with their entry to the Golden Lane Estate competition in 1952, which encapsulated the emerging Brutalism. Rising quite literally from the rubble of a heavily bomb-damaged site, the project treated the city on its own terms, 'as found', rather than to be remade from the ground up. The stark rectilinear forms in rough, raw concrete stood in striking contrast to the soft and smoother Scandinavian-influenced Modernism of the Festival of Britain, which was staged the previous year and of which the Smithsons were notably critical. And then there was the first instance of 'streets in the sky' – wide decks open to the elements from where each flat was accessed and which, it was hoped, would replicate the vibrant social life of the street.

In the end, the proposal by Geoffry Powell was chosen as the competition winner, and he went into partnership with Peter 'Joe'

Chamberlin and Christoph Bon to realise it. Although the latter parts of the estate were more obviously Brutalist – a prelude to the partnership's work at the adjacent Barbican – early phases are more in a Scandinavian and Corbusian idiom.

Despite this false start, Brutalist architecture would soon begin to spring up all over London, both as a consequence of bomb damage and the resulting acute housing shortage, and through modernisation programmes as a manifestation of the renewed national self-confidence of the 1960s. But, as we will see, it was frequently manifest in surprising and paradoxical ways.

Council housing is predictably where most Brutalism is to be found. But, while there are plenty of examples by architects working for the fabled London County Council architects' department, and later for boroughs, notably Camden and Lambeth, some of the most celebrated projects were by architects working in private practice, allocated work when the in-house public sector architects were overloaded. Then there is the seeming anomaly that the Barbican, the most famous housing project of the era, was not council housing at all but privately rented. And while this book contains many examples of schools, libraries, university and civic buildings, Brutalism in London and elsewhere was never straightforwardly the architecture of the welfare state. The simplistic narrative sometimes put forward that this was radical architecture reflecting radical social policy does not, moreover, account for the many examples of Brutalist commercial development. Nor does it reflect the way Brutalism was, counterintuitively, often deployed for new buildings by avowedly establishment institutions, from royal colleges to an ancient City of London livery company. Radical architecture, it would seem, was sometimes used for conservative ends.

Then there is the further paradox that if the New Brutalism of the 1950s was a distinctly English phenomenon, then the Brutalist architecture that arose across London during the following decades was as much, if not more so, part of the global movement that Brutalism had become – or rather, that had arisen in different parts of the world. This was especially the case when it came to urban planning policies, notably the influential idea that modern cities required a network of urban motorways. It is important to note that these planning policies were not in themselves Brutalist, and in many ways were in opposition to its chief tenets, but they were, nevertheless, frequently delivered and manifested through Brutalist architecture. In the end, in London, as in many other cities, only fragments of what was planned were ultimately realised, which today stand as ghosts of a future that never came to pass.

This apparent overreach and the popular opposition it provoked in London, most notably in Covent Garden, marked the beginning of the end of Brutalism and the social-democratic political settlement it was deemed to represent. Within a few short years, Camden Council's celebrated architects' department, for example, went from designing Brutalist housing to working in a discernibly Postmodern idiom. Meanwhile, Brutalist housing came under concerted attack. Among the leading voices was Canadian sociologist Oscar Newman, whose 'defensible space' theory saw Modernist design principles as playing an active role in crime and anti-social behaviour, ideas that he propounded to a BBC TV audience while touring the Aylesbury Estate for a 1974 documentary. This mantle was then picked up by geographer Alice Coleman in her book *Utopia on Trial* (1985) where, encoded in pseudo-scientific analysis, she took aim at the whole political edifice that Brutalism was deemed to represent.

The reaction against Modern architecture in general, and Brutalism in particular, only hardened during the 1990s, as footage of crowds cheering when tower blocks were dynamited became a regular feature of local news bulletins. In a country whose identity is arguably defined by nostalgia, it was perhaps obvious that as Britain emerged from the recession of the early 1990s and began once again to feel confident about its place in the world, it would look back to the 1960s, the previous moment when Britain had reached a cultural zenith and 'Swinging London' was the centre of the world. Though in the haze of Britpop and Cool Britannia, architecture was strangely absent. It seemingly went unnoticed that the exactly contemporary backdrop of The Kinks's 'Waterloo Sunset' was in fact the Brutalist Southbank Centre. Brutalism, it would seem, was still far too ridden with discredited politics to be appropriated in the way that popular music, for instance, had been. Indeed, Brutalism became the image of policies that were deemed to have palpably failed, with the Aylesbury Estate providing the location of Tony Blair's first speech after being elected in which he declared 'There will be no forgotten people in the Britain I want to build.'

Fast forward to the present and Brutalism has, if not been rehabilitated, then begun to be appreciated by a growing number of observers and aficionados. It is no coincidence that this change began in the aftermath of the 2008 financial crisis, when Brutalism began to be (re)discovered by a generation coming of age amidst economic turmoil and in search of evidence of political alternatives. And, of course, Brutalism's revival would not have proceeded the way it has without the rise of social media, where Brutalism's intrinsic 'imagistic' quality, which Banham identified half a century before, has led to a multitude of accounts dealing in moody black-and-white photographs of raw concrete.

Sensing which way the wind was blowing, even the National Trust – Britain's custodian of country houses and natural landscape – got in on the act in 2014, when it opened a 'pop-up' property at Balfron Tower. For two weeks visitors were able to explore flat 130 – the same flat where Ernő Goldfinger and his wife Ursula lived for two months after the building's completion – which had been furnished in 1960s style by designers Wayne

Hemingway and his daughter Tilly. There were many ironies here: the first was that the National Trust had taken over the flat after the building had been 'decanted' of council tenants prior to its refurbishment for private sale. Second was the fact that Balfron Tower had been deemed worthy of becoming heritage, while in its shadow stood the Smithsons' equally significant Robin Hood Gardens, which was slated for demolition.

To compound the bitter irony, when demolition finally began at Robin Hood Gardens in 2018, it transpired that the V&A Museum had acquired a section of the western block and was planning to display it in an exhibition later in the year at the Venice Architecture Biennale. That a building deemed unworthy of preserving as housing – and which had been neglected for years in anticipation of its demolition, despite people still living there – was at the same time considered significant enough to enter a museum collection and be preserved for posterity was, for many, hard to stomach. Seemingly caught unawares by the furore that this generated, the V&A professed their intention to start a debate about the future of council housing, even though such a debate had been raging for decades. The fragment now stands within the new V&A Storehouse in Stratford, returned to East London, yet sitting uneasily within the museum collection.

■ ■ ■ ■

How we see Brutalism today is as complicated and paradoxical as the movement itself – and this book reflects that. It features 58 buildings and developments from across London, ranging in type, scale, ambition and reputation. It includes only buildings that still exist, so there remains a void – just as there is in the city itself – of what has been lost. Like those examples consigned to the wrecking ball, of those that do still survive some are familiar, some are lesser known, a few are hardly known at all. Many are very well-documented, while for others there is a scarcity of information. As a result, the 58 buildings are explored in this book in different ways: some entries focus on the architect's intentions and the broader contexts from which the building emerged, others take a formal or stylistic analysis. The hope is that the diversity of approach reflects the diversity of Brutalist London itself. Although Brutalism has a number of defining traits and characteristics, there are different ways for a building to be Brutalist and in this book we see how Brutalism shapes, and is in turn shaped by, the surrounding city.

Returning to where we began, if we were to situate Brutalism in relation to the broader Modern Movement, it would be its Baroque phase, the final step in its stylistic evolution, where formal and structural principles are pushed to – and in some instances beyond – their limits. In retrospect, it's no surprise really that it was Brutalism and not earlier forms of Modernism that emerged and took such hold in London, a city still presided over by the masterpieces of Christopher Wren and Nicholas Hawksmoor, architects who were similarly energised by building in a city on the cusp of transformation.

Like the work of those heroes of the English Baroque, Brutalism is an architecture, above all, of power and drama. It is infused with energy – quite literally given the carbon footprint of all that concrete – that tries to reconcile with sheer mass and formal brio the contradictions that threatened to rip it apart: the very idea that architecture alone has the power to bring about social, cultural, even political transformation of a city. Brutalism did not shy away from these contradictions, or revel in them as Postmodernists would, but sought to grapple with and attempt to reconcile them. However flawed this endeavour, the buildings that resulted stand as physical evidence of a world shaped by a political settlement fundamentally different to our own, and as evidence that things could be different again.

List of buildings

01 Acland Burghley School
02 Alexandra Road Estate
03 Alton Estate
04 Ashington House
05 Balfron Tower; Carradale House; Glenkerry House
06 Barbican Estate
07 Bethnal Green Fire Station
08 Blackheath Meeting House
09 Brixton Recreation Centre
10 Brunel University Lecture Centre
11 Brunswick Centre
12 Camberwell Submarine
13 Centre Point
14 Chartered Accountants' Hall Extension
15 Church of St Paul's Bow Common
16 Cotton Gardens Estate
17 Crescent House, Golden Lane Estate
18 Dowgate Fire Station
19 Elephant and Rhinoceros Pavilion
20 Embassies of Czech and Slovak Republics (formerly Embassy of Czechoslovakia)
21 Eros House
22 Haggerston Girls' School
23 Hendon Hall Court
24 Housden House
25 Hyde Park Barracks
26 Institute of Education
27 Keeling House

28 Kensington and Chelsea Town Hall
29 Lambeth Road Police Control Centre
30 Lambeth Towers
31 Langham House Close
32 Lillington Gardens Estate
33 Ministry of Justice Offices (formerly the Home Office)
34 Minories Car Park
35 National Archives at Kew
36 National Theatre
37 Paddington British Rail Maintenance Depot
38 Perronet House
39 Royal College of Art, Darwin Building
40 Royal College of Physicians
41 Royal National Theatre Studio (formerly Old Vic Theatre Annexe)
42 Salters' Hall
43 SOAS Library
44 Southbank Centre: Queen Elizabeth Hall, Purcell Room and Hayward Gallery
45 Southwyck House
46 St Giles Hotel
47 Standard Hotel (formerly Camden Town Hall Annexe)
48 Stoke Newington School
49 Strand Building; Macadam Building, King's College
50 Sulkin House; Trevelyan House
51 Thamesmead
52 Travelodge Covent Garden
53 Trellick Tower
54 University of Westminster
55 Weeks Hall, Imperial College
56 Weston Rise Estate
57 Whittington Estate
58 World's End Housing

Acland Burghley School

Howell, Killick, Partridge & Amis (HKPA), 1963-66
93 Burghley Road, NW5 1UJ

When the London County Council architects' department had too much work, they had a list of approved private practices who would be allocated projects they couldn't accommodate in-house. This was how Howell, Killick, Partridge & Amis (HKPA) got the commission to design a new building for the amalgamated Acland and Burghley schools, located on the site of the latter in Tufnell Park.

The brief was for a 1,320-place comprehensive school (the London County Council was a pioneer of non-selective education) with the need for flexibility to allow for later changes in education organisation. The existing buildings needed to stay in use until the new building was fully complete.

Their solution was a modular plan. The three main teaching blocks for the lower, middle and upper schools radiate out to the east from a central core, with a longer range connecting to its north, running east to west. This would later connect to the sports hall and art block. The overall forms are stark: the teaching blocks are stacked boxes with angular stair towers, the core a kinked oblong, the linear range a truncated wedge, and the main entrance a drawbridge-like ramp. But the handling of the materials – a combination of cast-in-place and precast concrete with a flint-faced exterior – while robust, has a deftness and attention to detail that unfolds through daily use. This is especially the case in the adjoining hexagonal assembly hall, with its fair-faced concrete frame, clerestory windows and timber-clad ceiling.

Alexandra Road Estate

Neave Brown, 1972–78
Rowley Way, NW8

At the conclusion of his sell-out 'in conversation' at Hackney Empire in October 2017, Neave Brown received a standing ovation lasting no less than 10 minutes. Not long before, he had received the Royal Gold Medal – one of architecture's highest accolades. It was a remarkable turnaround for an architect who had built little over a career spent largely in local authority architects' departments. Yet, it was entirely fitting given the way Brown combined formal invention with a profound sense of humanity – exemplified in his masterwork, Alexandra Road.

The site was not a promising one: a long sliver of land hard up against the mainline railway. Brown's solution was to use what others might have seen as an irresolvable encumbrance to his advantage. He conceived a linear composition rising to eight storeys that hugs the railway line on one side, while on the other it steps down, a form repeated by the opposing smaller block, creating a kind of concrete valley around a pedestrianised street that runs its length.

The result is a vigorous, sculptural composition that at the same time supports a vivid social and street life. The dwellings have decent-sized balconies and are accessed by a front door that opens to the outside – in contrast to the internal lobbies of many of the point and slab blocks that had defined the previous decade. Acknowledging and reworking traditional terrace typologies, Alexandra Road is a bold expression of the power of council housing to enrich the city – socially, materially and culturally.

Alton Estate

London County Council Architects' Department, 1951–59
Roehampton, SW15

'Throughout the industrial revolution people have been trying to escape from the slums and architects have been dreaming of cities in the sky, cities and towers amongst green landscape. What we see here on the edge of Richmond Park is probably the most exciting statement of that utopian ideal.' This is how Richard Rogers described the Alton Estate in a 1996 BBC programme. Over 60 years since the estate's completion, it's still hard to disagree.

The Alton Estate was the London County Council's first opportunity to design not just housing, but a whole community, with schools, shops and communal buildings. The estate is in two parts: East and West. The first to be constructed was East, designed by a team led by Rosemary Stjernstedt, and drawing from Scandinavian precedent with its point towers and blocks clad in brick. A particularly English characteristic of the estate is the setting in the 18th-century landscape that the planners had retained. So, rather than rising in a desolate landscape of featureless grass, as was the case with many estates of this period, the buildings were set on sloping ground, surrounded by large trees.

This was the same for the slightly later, larger and much more Brutalist Alton West. Here, the influences were strongly Corbusian, especially the Unité d'Habitation, yet it remains attuned to the landscape, with an almost Georgian-inspired geometrical configuration of the blocks' concrete grids and their elevation on *pilotis* allowing the landscape to flow underneath. It is utopian indeed.

ASHINGTON HOUSE

Ashington House

Noel Moffett Associates, 1970–74
Somerford Street, E1 5RE

Ashington House is technically part of the Collingwood Estate, which occupies a large area to the west of Cambridge Heath Road. The estate rose from a major 'slum clearance' during the 1920s and was largely complete within the decade. Architecturally it is polite if rather dull: several storeys of brick with pitched roofs, some Neo-Georgian detailing here and there.

Ashington House itself could not be more different: a dynamic mass of stacked and layered cuboids of brick with concrete bases, loosely and rather irregularly stepping back from the garden square around which it is arranged. Designed by Noel Moffett Associates for the Greater London Council, it was a response to not just the surrounding estate, but also much of the council housing that had gone up in the East End and elsewhere during the preceding decades: mostly point blocks and overly scaled slabs, where individual residences are subsumed into the faceless mass. Here, however, the individual flats have an identity and legibility within the collective whole, while urbanistically, the overall composition has a far more animated and engaging presence, a building that is part of the city rather than trying to reinvent – both classically Brutalist characteristics.

The robustness of materials is countered by the balconies and roof gardens – amenities for residents and also where they can stamp their personalities on the block. Complementing the composition are elegant hexagonally planned two-storey houses for disabled and elderly residents.

Balfron Tower; Carradale House; Glenkerry House

Ernő Goldfinger, 1965–75
St Leonard's Road, E14

In a city now full of towers competing for attention, Balfron Tower remains one of the most distinctive high-rise buildings in London. Standing 26 storeys tall, it was designed, along with the adjoining lower-rise Carradale House and Glenkerry House, by the Hungarian emigré architect Ernő Goldfinger. Trained in the pre-war High Modernist style, Goldfinger was by the 1960s an avowed Brutalist, combining striking concrete forms with progressive social programmes.

Conceived as a community in the sky, Balfron contains 146 flats and maisonettes, with the accommodation block offset by an adjoining service tower containing the lift shafts and topped by a boiler room. The two towers are connected by walkways daringly suspended in mid-air. These align to the lift stops at every third floor. Goldfinger's intention with this arrangement was both practical and social: reducing construction costs and saving time in everyday use, while consolidating the entrances for three floors of flats onto one walkway created more opportunities for the type of social interaction that towers were often accused of eliminating.

The flats themselves are well arranged and proportioned, something that Goldfinger had direct experience of having spent several weeks living in one of the flats with his wife Ursula soon after the building's completion, during which time they hosted champagne receptions for residents.

Scandalously, in the mid-2010s, council tenants were decanted and the flats were refurbished for private sale.

BALFRON TOWER

Barbican Exhibition Halls

Barbican Estate

Chamberlin, Powell & Bon, 1963-82
Silk Street, EC2Y 8BA

The name Barbican – technically a medieval defensive structure – is an incongruous one for London's greatest Brutalist set-piece. Arranged over an area of the city that was laid waste in the Blitz, the Barbican is classically Modernist in its vertical separation of traffic and pedestrians via a vast multi-level podium and its incorporation of different components in a single megastructure. The three residential towers signal its presence on the skyline. Although identical in their triangular plan and nearly in height (at 43 storeys, Cromwell Tower has one floor fewer than the others), their varying rotations make them appear quite different.

The towers rise amid a configuration of courts and crescents, which in plan recall Georgian precedents, but in experience feel like stepping into a 1970s sci-fi film, with the lakes, cascading water and gardens. Overall, the complex accommodates 6,500 people in 2,113 flats that deploy 140 different plans. This is a far cry from the standardised mass housing generally associated with the era. At its core is an internationally renowned arts centre, with its concert hall, theatre, art gallery and cinemas.

The architectural language stands apart from more conventional Modernist approaches in its overt massiveness, with bush-hammered piers and beams on a gargantuan scale. Beyond this, and in contrast to the futuristic feel, there are a number of medieval allusions – arrow-slit windows, ramparts and massive Romanesque piers – which have the appearance of serving to keep the city out, which is one of the main criticisms levelled at the complex.

art galler

Bethnal Green Fire Station

Greater London Council Architects' Department, 1966-67
11 Roman Road, E2 0HU

A fire station has stood on the site on the north side of Roman Road since 1871. A grand Victorian building opened in 1889 and was then enlarged in 1906. This building had served as the local firefighting hub during the Blitz, but by the 1960s it was deemed out of date, with the current station built a few doors down to replace it.

Ostensibly, there is little in common between the Neo-Gothic forerunner and its Brutalist replacement. While the previous building is five storeys, with tall chimney stacks and originally an even taller octagonal tower, the new building is low – just two storeys. At ground level are three large bays for the fire engines. Narrow concrete verticals demarcate the openings while tracing a line to the first floor, which projects above. The composition is crisp and rectilinear, with neat bands of concrete supporting corresponding bands of brown brick and an off-centre oriel window punctuating the street elevation. The visual and material language extends to the adjoining accommodation, which continues up Victoria Park Square to the west, and the training tower to the east, which is cleverly and unusually brought into the whole composition.

Despite their obvious differences, both the Victorian and Brutalist fire stations have a robustness to them – buildings designed to be heavily used – and a clear civic presence connoting their role in serving the city.

Blackheath Meeting House

Trevor Dannatt & Partners, 1971-72
Lawn Terrace, SE3 9LL

Brutalist architecture can be abrasive – literally and figuratively – but it can also be gentle, sensitive and welcoming, as it was in the hands of Trevor Dannatt. Part of the team of architects responsible for the Royal Festival Hall, Dannatt is renowned for his intelligent, carefully crafted and, ultimately, humane interpretation of Modernism, of which the Blackheath Meeting House is a finely wrought example.

Born and raised in Blackheath, Dannatt was the obvious choice as an architect of a meeting house for the Society of Friends – commonly known as Quakers – when a plot adjacent to the Blackheath Congregational Church (where they had met in the basement and which Dannatt had rebuilt in 1957) became available. Square in plan with chamfered corners, the meeting house is set back and at an angle to the adjoining road. Externally, one is met by angled walls of concrete topped by a square lantern, with the ground floor set back into a wall of glazing behind a single faceted column. Entering the building, the effect is more modest, almost domestic in its quiet, unassuming quality.

Inside, Dannatt worked with the leading engineer Ted Happold to design a timber and steel tie-beam ceiling that, through a clever engineering solution, has the effect of floating over the space below. In its form and materials, the building both stands apart and blends into its surroundings – a composition of gentle monumentality.

Brixton Recreation Centre
Brixton Recreation
SAM CENTER
HERBAL TOWN
Dr Deng
Free Consultation
Acupuncture
Chinese Medicine
THE LOC BAR
36
CCTV

Brixton Recreation Centre

George Finch and Ted Hollamby, 1975-85
27 Brixton Station Road, SW9 8QQ

Brixton Recreation Centre was to be the centrepiece of a wholesale redevelopment of Brixton Town Centre. The design was entrusted by Lambeth's director of architecture, Ted Hollamby, to George Finch. An accomplished housing architect, Finch had no experience of leisure centres, so he undertook extensive research, visiting facilities across the country.

Brixton Rec, as it is known, would be on an altogether different scale and ambition from almost all contemporary examples, encompassing three swimming pools, two cafés, squash courts, bowls halls, sports hall, gymnasium, restaurant, bar and even a disco. This almost megastructure-like building was conceived as a new part of the city that would integrate with a planned elevated walkway system, but deploying a material palette that drew from its existing surroundings: red brick, copper roof and concrete – in place of stone – for the heroic piers and escape stairs.

Inside, a central atrium slices vertically through the building, giving a clear sense of openness and legibility to a complex programme. All the interiors are conceived with creativity and care, but the real highlight (along with the atrium) is the main swimming pool, with its timber-lined saw-tooth roof.

Memories of being behind schedule and over budget vanished as the building quickly became the heart of the community. It was famously visited by Nelson Mandela on his first state visit in 1996.

Brixton Recreation Centre
Brixton Rec
RED SEA
PEDESTRIAN ZONE
No vehicles
Mon - Sun
8 am - 6 pm
BRIXTON STATION ROAD
POPE'S ROAD
Except cycles
ACTIVE LAMBETH
Recreation Centre
Gym
Swimming Pool
Sports Hall
Family Leisure Zone
Café
Birthday Parties
Conference Room
Squash Courts
Boxing
Nursery

LM72 NYD

Brunel University Lecture Centre

Richard Sheppard, Robson & Partners, 1965–66
Kingston Lane, Uxbridge, UB8 3PH

In 1963, the Robbins Report into higher education was published. Its principal recommendation was an expansion of higher education and the conversion of technical colleges into full universities. Among the latter would be the College of Advanced Technology in Acton, for which plans were already being developed to move to a larger, purpose-built site near Uxbridge.

Richard Sheppard was commissioned to draw up a masterplan and oversee the design of a number of buildings. At the heart of the new campus was the Lecture Centre, which houses six separate lecture theatres in addition to various teaching spaces. Lecture theatres had long offered modern architects intriguing formal and structural possibilities, from Konstantin Melnikov's Constructivist Rusakov Workers' Club in Moscow to Stirling and Gowan's Leicester Engineering Building. Here, Sheppard Robson's project architect, John Heywood, took his chance and designed an immensely powerful configuration, all in raw concrete, of two rows of three lecture theatres stacked onto each other, with escape stairs left unglazed and the upper layer daringly cantilevered out. The result is to give the composition a powerful civic presence as the centrepiece of the campus and the sunken square on which it looks out.

Turning the corner, one sees the angled profile of the raked seating, which is then bookended by circular stair towers, before the language becomes less dramatic, though no less geometrically rigorous, in the classroom wing.

Lecture Centre
Quad South

No loading
At any time

Brunswick Centre

Patrick Hodgkinson, 1961-66; completed by TP Bennett & Partners, 1967-72
Bernard Street, WC1N

At first glance, the Brunswick Centre has little in common with its surroundings amid the polite terraces of Bloomsbury. It comprises two longitudinal blocks, ziggurat-shaped in section, facing one another across a linear shopping precinct. The end to the south is left open, while that to the north is enclosed by a supermarket. All told, it contains 560 flats, with accommodation for 1,644 people. These are mostly one- and two-bedroom residences – each with a balcony off the heavily glazed main living space. Access is generally via internal walkways, where one finds oneself walking amid a vertebrae-like series of piers and buttresses. It is sculpturally invigorating, though not especially homely. Below are around 80 retail units, a cinema and a car park with space for nearly 1,000 cars.

Externally, four service towers on each side punctuate the rhythm of the alternating paired bays of glazing and balconies. In the abstract, the resultant effect has faint echoes of the surrounding Georgian and Victorian terraces. This would have been accentuated by Hodgkinson's proposed stucco-like cream paint scheme, which was never completed.

The shopping precinct underwent extensive refurbishment in the late 2000s, transforming it from a windswept and often bleak space into one bustling with people. Sadly, the familiar chain stores and restaurants have replaced the idiosyncratic businesses that had grown up over the decades.

Warning

Camberwell Submarine

Ted Hollamby and Bill Jacoby, 1973–74
Akerman Road, SW9 7BD

Among London's more curious architectural typologies are the columns, statues and even small temples that actually serve as ventilation shafts for the tube tunnels, car parks, underpasses, sewers and other bits of infrastructure that occupy the ground below. But the most dramatic by far is the 'Camberwell Submarine' that rises to the surface on Akerman Road in south London. Rather than try to hide away, this is a celebration of the communal heating that fed the surrounding Myatts Field North housing estate, of which it is the last surviving element.

Designed under the oversight of Ted Hollamby, Lambeth's director of architecture, Myatts Field North was a low-rise estate reflecting the turn away from high-rise living that began in the 1960s. It comprised a range of interconnected blocks linked by a combination of ground-level paths and elevated walkways, in yellow London stock brick with slate roofs. Like the decision to build low rather than high, the choice of traditional materials again reflected a desire to adhere more closely to traditional housing typologies. The submarine stood apart, therefore, as a wonderfully sculptural and avowedly Brutalist statement in concrete.

Today, the submarine sits amid the so-called Oval Quarter – a privately financed development that replaced the Myatts Field North estate with terraces. Unusually for a privatised scheme, it made use of the district heating system, with the submarine's turrets extended by four metres as a result.

ON
SECURE

Centre Point

Richard Seifert, 1961-66
101-103 New Oxford Street, WC1A 1DB

Brutalism is often seen as having little to do with refinement – and with good reason. For many of its best-known proponents it was about being bold and brash, revelling in raw surfaces. But at Centre Point we see how a Brutalist building can be smooth, polished, elegant in form and in detail – a refinement that served as a decoy for the hard-headed commercialism of its architect, Richard Seifert, and the take-no-prisoners approach of its developer, Harry Hyams.

Hyams had acquired a number of plots at St Giles Circus in central London, with a view to undertaking a large-scale development. But it was Seifert who unlocked its potential by convincing the London County Council to loosen their height restrictions in return for some of the site being set aside for road usage, to help traffic flow in this notoriously congested part of London. Seifert was able to get an office tower of 33 storeys – then Britain's tallest – with an adjoining block of eight storeys containing further offices, retail and some housing – all raised up on sculptural *pilotis*. The design was the responsibility of George Marsh, who devised a concept of precast concrete T-frames, which were then stacked to create the building's elegant form, enlivened by the frame's chamfered edges.

Hyams notoriously kept the building vacant for several years after its completion to try to sign up a single tenant on a long lease, sparking protests from housing campaigners. Today, the building has been converted into private housing but remains largely unoccupied.

Chartered Accountants' Hall Extension

William Whitfield, 1966–70
11 Copthall Avenue, EC2R 7EF

Brutalism is by its very definition uncompromising. So, it would seem unsuited to settings where sensitivity is usually required, such as when adding to or adapting historic buildings. But when that building is one of the most powerful and full-blooded examples of the Edwardian Baroque in London, then what could be more appropriate?

That building was the Institute of Chartered Accountants, designed by John Belcher and his pupil Arthur Beresford Pite, with a 1930 extension in the same style by Belcher's later partner, JJ Joass. Comprising two frontages facing Moorgate Place and Great Swan Alley, the design is a masterwork of exaggerated ornamentation and Michelangelo-inspired Mannerism, with sculpture by the renowned Hamo Thornycroft and others.

When he was commissioned to extend the building once again in 1959, William Whitfield's response was both continuity and radical departure. His first move was to continue Joass's extension around the corner onto Copthall Avenue, where he built an additional entrance portal. Then alongside this, he created a strongly vertical composition of concrete and glass, powerfully articulating the substantial insertion of five office floors and the new Great Hall, the massive transverse beams of which cantilever out of Langthorn Court to the north. Up close, the careful detailing and articulation of materials becomes apparent. Though it remains a bold statement, it is nevertheless highly appropriate in continuing the spirit (if not the architectural language) of the original building.

Church of St Paul's Bow Common

Robert Maguire and Keith Murray, 1956-60
Burdett Road, E3 4AR

'Truly this is none other but the House of God. This is the gate of heaven.' These words from the Book of Genesis in bold lettering designed by Ralph Beyer adorn the small octagonal porch that leads worshippers into the Church of St Paul's Bow Common. With the exception of this lettering, the exterior of the church is unadorned and austere. Large expanses of brown brick face the rectangular low level, which is animated only by the zigzag concrete roof. The brick facing continues above with another higher rectangular form set back. And then, set behind this is a glazed pyramid-topped lantern – its lightness, in every sense of the word, contrasting with the dark heaviness below.

Inside, the deliberately low and consequently dark entrance area gives way to the brightness of the central space, lit by triangular clerestory windows and the lantern above. The church was pioneering in its centralised planning in England, developing the principles of the Liturgical Movement that sought to bring priest and congregation together. Thus, the altar is in the centre of the church, under a stripped-back baldacchino and steel corona hanging around it. The overall effect is one of contrasts: between darkness and austerity and the lightness and comparative finesse of the lantern; and between inside and outside – a church designed to keep the city out, a space, as the words on the exterior make clear, conceived as an otherworldly haven.

THIS IS THE GA

E OF HEAVEN

Cotton Gardens Estate

George Finch, 1968
Kennington Lane, SE11

Prefabricated concrete panels have a bad reputation – technically and aesthetically – and frequently result in featureless monotony. Not at Cotton Gardens. Here, George Finch created a composition full of energy and dynamism, showing the potential of concrete panel construction to create architecture that's vigorous and distinctive, and encapsulates its socially transformative potential.

The son of a milkman, Finch was born in Tottenham and began his architectural training not far away at North London Polytechnic (now London Metropolitan University). But it was at the Architectural Association where he found a socially minded ambition that matched his own. From there, he joined the London County Council's housing division and then, in 1963, the new Lambeth Borough Council architects' department under the leadership of Ted Hollamby. Housing was inevitably the department's main focus, and Finch's experience and ingenuity saw him become one of Hollamby's most trusted lieutenants.

One of the very many clever aspects of Finch's design for Cotton Gardens is the fact that the three towers are identical, but through their orientation and powerful composition retain an individual quality – one of the reasons, other than their obvious quality, that the design was later utilised elsewhere in Lambeth. At ground level, the towers are integrated with a doctors' surgery and community centre, surrounded by landscaped play areas, all components of Finch's vision of an egalitarian and socially inclusive society.

BARBICAN
CARPET&FLOORING
H

Crescent House, Golden Lane Estate

Chamberlin, Powell & Bon, 1958-62
Goswell Road, EC1Y

Following the Second World War, the population remaining in the City of London could be counted in the hundreds. Eager to stem the tide of depopulation, the Corporation of London embarked on a project to build a housing estate on land to the north of Cripplegate. An architectural competition was held in 1951, which was won by the young architect Geoffry Powell, who had agreed with his colleagues Peter 'Joe' Chamberlin and Christoph Bon to enter a partnership to deliver the project should any of them be successful.

Over the following years, the partnership would oversee the well-ordered design of a series of housing blocks arranged around courtyards and hard landscaping, complemented by amenities such as a nursery, community centre and swimming pool. Its centrepiece was the 16-storey Great Arthur House – an elegant tower with a striking yellow curtain wall, concrete balconies and a flamboyant butterfly structure at its top that serves to hide the water tanks.

The last phase of the project was Crescent House, along Goswell Road. Here, the largely pre-war Modernist styling of the rest of the estate gives way to a much more explicitly Brutalist architectural language, inspired by Le Corbusier's Maisons Jaoul (1953–55). The flats are articulated as rectilinear projections from a thick concrete base raised up on *pilotis* and topped by a segmental arched arcade that prefigures ideas the partnership would soon develop for the adjacent Barbican.

LFB
LONDON FIRE BRIGADE
Dowgate Fire Station &
Fire Investigation Team
www.london-fire.gov.uk

Dowgate Fire Station

Hubbard Ford & Partners, 1975
94–95 Upper Thames Street, EC4R 3UE

'To me this building is redolent of a word processor' was how the then Prince Charles described Mondial House, which stood on the riverfront next to Cannon Street Station from the mid-1970s to 2006. Those commuters walking over London Bridge who saw its extraordinary stepped ziggurat forms and dramatic black-and-white banding rising up would be hard pressed to disagree with the prince's characterisation. Yet its appearance made a great deal of sense when one realised it was a telephone exchange inhabited not by humans, but by whirring machines that connected Londoners to a global telephone network (a clue was in its name). The subsequent advent of digitisation meant that infrastructure could be miniaturised, making these often vast structures redundant, and because of their peculiar type, they were not adaptable to other uses.

So, in 2006, Mondial House came down, but not entirely. In its north-west corner was Dowgate Fire Station, which was required to remain operational, with the structure retained now acting as a podium to a box of offices above. One interesting feature is that in contrast to the sharp angles one often associates with Brutalism, the various apertures for doors, windows and the large openings for the fire engine feature elegantly rounded corners, accentuated by the detailing with fair-faced edges, all of which gives the building a futuristic feel. It is a testament to its power that this fragment can conjure a sense of the much larger complex it was once a part of.

Elephant and Rhinoceros Pavilion

Casson, Conder & Partners, 1962-65
London Zoo, Regent's Park, NW1 4RY

London Zoo is not just a menagerie of animals but of architecture, home to important examples of pre-war purism, proto-High Tech and, in the form of Hugh Casson and Neville Conder's Elephant and Rhinoceros Pavilion, sculptural Brutalism.

Casson and Conder are generally seen as establishment Modernists rather than Brutalists. Casson had been director of architecture of the Festival of Britain, which many paid-up Brutalists had been critical of, and later designed the refined interiors of the Royal Yacht Britannia. Yet, when they came to design the Elephant and Rhinoceros Pavilion – with Casson doing initial sketches and Conder as principal designer – Brutalism was the route they chose.

The project formed part of a development plan the duo had drawn up for the Zoo in 1956, and like other Modernist buildings on the site it draws formal inspiration from the animals it was designed to house. The irregular cluster of vertical cylindrical forms topped by pointed copper roofs is derived from the way elephants and rhinoceroses huddle together in the wild while drinking. The grey striated concrete exterior echoes the colour and texture of their skin, while being strong enough to withstand one of the large animals rubbing up against it. The public spaces inside are robust like the exterior, but rather less Brutalist in their form and materials.

Despite its inspiration from the animals it was intended to house, the Elephant and Rhinoceros Pavilion is no longer used for its original purpose.

Embassies of Czech and Slovak Republics (formerly Embassy of Czechoslovakia)

Jan Bočan, Robert Matthew, Johnson-Marshall & Partners, Jan Šrámek and Karel Štěpánský, 1965–70
25, 26–30 Kensington Palace Gardens, W8 4QY

Walking north along Kensington Palace Gardens, the row of large Italianate villas (now often housing embassies) suddenly gives way to an extraordinary Brutalist composition as one approaches Notting Hill Gate. This is the first of two buildings built for the Embassy of Czechoslovakia – which now houses the separate embassies of the Czech and Slovak Republics.

The pavilion on Kensington Palace Gardens, which is actually the less prominent of the two given the heavy passing traffic on Notting Hill Gate, is a four-storey composition of raw concrete panels. Square in plan, and originally holding the ambassador's office, the building is composed as a rectilinear grid, the regular rhythm of which it playfully subverts into a syncopation of solids, voids and uprights. Floating apparently effortlessly above the ground, the angled recessions of the glazing (and projecting side elevation) give the building an oddly ethereal quality, with the projections and recessions casting long beautiful shadows.

Turning the corner is the larger and seemingly more everyday slab block of seven storeys, which originally had accommodation for embassy officials above consulate offices at ground floor. But closer inspection shows similar sophistication and, at times, a quite sculptural handling of materials and detailing. While ostensibly a departure from the surrounding buildings, there are gentle Classical allusions even here, in the ordered composition and the quasi-rustication of the ground-floor uprights.

LC18 PPY

Eros House

Rodney Gordon for Owen Luder Partnership, 1960–63
Brownhill Road, SE6 2EG

Eros House is unusual among Owen Luder Partnership's major projects for the simple fact that it's still standing, albeit in an altered and dilapidated condition. Designed by Luder's chief designer Rodney Gordon, Eros House is a residential tower of nine storeys – one of the first properly Brutalist towers in London or indeed the UK. The essentially rectilinear geometric form of the main block is animated by alternating projections and recessions of the paired window arrangement. The supporting stair tower, with its angled concrete structure and near-flush glazing, exhibits similar Constructivist angularity to Stirling and Gowan's almost exactly contemporary Leicester Engineering Building, albeit in more modest form. The stunning raw concrete spiral stair at the rear prefigures Luder and Gordon's even more sculptural Trinity Square in Gateshead and Tricorn Centre in Portsmouth – both now demolished.

Sadly, the windows of the main block have been overclad with plastic, though fortunately the tower survives with its original glazing. A few years after Eros House's completion, Luder returned to the site to design Milford Towers (1969–74) across the road – a series of interconnected blocks of council housing with a shopping centre underneath, demonstrating an interesting evolution of his ideas. However, like Eros House, it is in a poor state of repair, with a certificate of immunity from listing having been issued in 2022.

Haggerston Girls' School

Ernő Goldfinger, 1964–67
Weymouth Terrace, E2 8LS

Haggerston Girls' School, now known as Haggerston School, was Ernő Goldfinger's only secondary school, though he did design two primary schools in the late 1940s and early 1950s. As the building's listing entry notes, Goldfinger's progression from designing for primary- to secondary-age students is mirrored in his stylistic progression as an architect, with Haggerston demonstrative of his later, fully Brutalist, phase.

Goldfinger conceived the school in three parts. At its core was the longitudinal teaching block, arranged as a rectilinear concrete grid 12 bays long. Circulation is provided by a central corridor. Bands of projecting glazing at the north-east and south-west ends of the building punctuate the grid, while denoting spaces for year groups and library and specialist teaching, respectively. The other two blocks are both square in plan, with the one to the east housing entrance spaces, an assembly hall and music rehearsal rooms, and the one to the west containing a gymnasium.

The school was sensitively refurbished in 2010–12 by Avanti Architects who, along with restoring a number of interiors, also designed an additional block in keeping with Goldfinger's original composition, which as a whole reflected his interests in integrating Classical design principles in Modernist architecture. Intriguingly, despite the Brutalist appearance, the elevations follow the golden section, while the concrete frame's smooth uprights and textured horizontals, and the roof parapet can all be read in Classical terms.

Hendon Hall Court

Owen Luder, 1961–66
Parson Street, NW4 1QY

Hendon Hall Court lies in the grounds of Hendon Hall – an 18th-century manor house, latterly used as a hotel, with various 19th-century accretions, including an oversized portico that is possibly taken from Colen Campbell's demolished Wanstead House. It's hard to think of more incongruous neighbours.

Hendon Hall Court was Owen Luder's first independent project, having set up his own practice in 1957, and was also the first time he partnered with the developer Alec Colman, with whom he would build his most famous projects: Trinity Square in Gateshead and the Tricorn Centre in Portsmouth. In comparison to those large projects, Hendon Hall Court is relatively modest (and, perhaps for that reason, still standing).

It is composed as a long rectangular range, five storeys in height, containing 54 flats and maisonettes. Instead of standing as a single, monolithic slab, competing rhythms of recessions and projections in the gridded arrangement give the block real dynamism. This is accentuated by the recessed balconies, where solids are set alongside voids and vice versa, with further animation provided by the chamfering of the undersides of each balcony. A projecting entranceway is set off-centre, with a circulation core behind. Particularly dramatic is the side elevation, where the profile of the block is repeated in a projecting inner section.

The painting of the shuttered concrete has dulled the building's original effect somewhat, but it remains a powerful – and given the context somewhat unexpected – composition.

Housden House

Brian Housden, 1963-65
78 South Hill Park, NW3 2SN

The grand terraces overlooking Hampstead Ponds might be a surprising place to find a Modernist house, let alone a Brutalist one. But the house that Brian Housden built for himself and his family is far from the only one, with Goldfinger's 2 Willow Road nearby and houses by Stanley Amis and Bill Howell, who would later form HKPA, next door. But even this does not prepare one for the superabundant strangeness of the Housden House – part Gerrit Rietveld, part Aldo van Eyck, part Maison de Verre, maybe part MC Escher too.

The Dutch connotations are no coincidence as Housden and his wife had visited Holland after acquiring the site and actually met Truus Schröder-Schräder and Rietveld. From their famous 1924 house, Housden took the idea of architecture conceived as a series of interlocking planes and volumes. So, from South Hill Park, one approaches the house on what reveals itself as a kind of bridge with a lower-ground-floor patio below and projecting canopies above. Inside, the spaces are similarly layered and intersecting, with some rigidly defined and others flowing into one another vertically and horizontally – reflecting van Eyck's concept of a house being a landscape with furniture that was built into its fabric (other freestanding pieces were designed by Rietveld himself). Housden later wrote that a 'private house is a little city' – a description that could not be more fitting of his own complex and multilayered composition set above the landscape.

Hyde Park Barracks

Basil Spence & Partners, 1967–70
South Carriage Drive, SW7 1SE

Cavalry barracks have stood on the site next to Hyde Park since 1792, with Basil Spence's Brutalist barracks, which accommodate the Household Cavalry responsible for the guarding of Buckingham Palace, replacing those that were built at the end of the 19th century. There were many requirements in the brief: accommodation, messes, offices, recreational facilities, as well as stables and a riding school. Spence's response was a complex of buildings, utilising the concrete segmental arch as a recurring structural device and motif, which is set against red brick walls and a leaded roof in a way that recalls Le Corbusier's Maisons Jaoul. In contrast to the uniformity one might expect from barracks, the combination of recessions and projections, and vertical and horizontal emphasis, give the blocks an irregular rhythm, breaking up the structure into a series of components, which include a gateway supporting a retained pediment from the previous Victorian building.

Rising amid the blocks appears something quite different: a tower just under 100 metres tall, which looms oddly over the adjacent park. Vertical fins run the tower's full height to give the composition a real vigour and elegantly culminate in a wonderfully sculptural arrangement that appears something like a concrete crown. Although sometimes criticised for the robustness of the design and the chosen materials, nothing could be more appropriate for Spence when conceiving a building that, after all, housed soldiers.

Institute of Education

Denys Lasdun & Partners, 1970–76
20 Bedford Way, WC1H 0AL

In 1959, the University of London published a development plan for its Bloomsbury site by the architects Leslie Martin and Trevor Dannatt. Building on the pre-war proposal by Charles Holden, which had yielded Senate House, the plan envisaged a university precinct articulated around a central 'spine' running north to south. On Martin and Dannatt's recommendation, Denys Lasdun, fresh from his work at the University of East Anglia (UEA), was appointed to work up detailed designs for a number of the buildings. However, by the mid-1960s, the tide was turning against the kind of wholesale redevelopment scheme Martin and Dannatt had proposed and, although protests against it were finally rejected in 1969, it was only partially realised over the following years, with Lasdun's Institute of Education the most significant element.

Like UEA, and the nearby Brunswick Centre (11), Lasdun's proposal was more megastructure than building: a long block running along Bedford Way, with five colossal service and circulation towers punctuating a lower, otherwise continuous run of dark glazing and spandrel panels emerging from a wide trench. The corners at the north and south ends are chiselled out to reveal skeletal concrete piers that denote the entrances. On the opposing side, a 'spur' steps out of one of the concrete service towers in a direct echo of UEA. The plan was for further spurs to the north, but the retention of terraces on Woburn Square left Lasdun's composition in truncated form.

17 Russell Square
FUEL
MY FUTURE
FOR THE
PRICE OF
A COFFEE?

Controlled
ZONE

Keeling House

Denys Lasdun of Fry, Drew, Drake & Lasdun, 1957-59
Claredale Street, E2 6PG

It is hard to imagine that Keeling House could be any more different than the rows of Victorian terraced houses that lie to its immediate south. Like the earlier prototypes on nearby Morpeth Street and Knottisford Street (50), Keeling House is a 'cluster block', that is a tight-angled arrangement of four accommodation towers around a central service and circulation tower. At 16 storeys, it was a relatively early example of high-rise council housing that was driven by the value seen in achieving densities on small footprints, thereby reducing the need for substantial site clearances.

Thus, a consequence of Keeling House's height was the preservation and intended refurbishment of surrounding streets. At the same time, its cluster arrangement emerged as a way of mitigating what were already identified as challenges with high-rise living, notably social disconnection. Residents enter the building together and pass communal spaces to get to their front doors. And, rather than flats, the blocks contain maisonettes suitable for a range of family units. (The one exception was a row of flats that appears after the first two rows of maisonettes creating a datum with the height of surrounding buildings.)

In its form, the building is pared back to a stark geometry of horizontals and verticals, accentuated by the intense contrasts between light and shade. In some ways, the building's aesthetic radicalism obscures the way it was actually conceived in relation to its surroundings.

Kensington and Chelsea Town Hall

Basil Spence, 1972–76
Hornton Street, W8 7NX

It seems surprising in retrospect to observe that just five years separate the completion of E Vincent Harris's politely Classical Central Library in 1960 and the conception of Basil Spence's mammoth Town Hall for the amalgamated borough of Kensington and Chelsea in 1965. The only indication that these two buildings exist in the same architectural worlds is that both occupy the same tightly constrained site and the common use of red brick. But where Harris's building is content to sit politely, Spence's building has a compressed, tightly wound feel.

Although designed in the 1960s, and a product of that decade in conception, Spence's Town Hall was begun in 1972 and only completed in 1976, ten days after the death of its architect at the age of 69. The building is composed as a series of semi-discrete components. To the south are two wings, square in plan with canted corners, set amid a courtyard. On the east is the council chamber, raised up on a concrete frame. On the west is the great hall, windowless and all of brick with the walls splaying out into the paving. Between the two wings is a balcony for the mayor to address the people, with the civic suite denoted by the oriel windows behind. The vast central block is square in plan but irregularly treated on all sides, though generally stepping back in deference to its surroundings. In the centre is a courtyard, with a giant redwood tree at its heart – a strangely calm and secluded foil to an otherwise restless composition.

YOUR LITTER PLEASE

LAMBETH ROAD

Lambeth Road Police Control Centre

Lambeth Architects' Department, 1966
109 Lambeth Road, SE1 7LP

On Lambeth Road is one of London's more enigmatic buildings. At first glance, the façade immediately facing the road appears wholly – perhaps deliberately – unremarkable. Closer inspection reveals a surprising geometrical and material sophistication: an initial stratum of brick followed by three levels of precast concrete panels, alternating with bands of glazing and exposed floor slab. The horizontality is balanced by vertical recessions, where pairs of supporting piers are exposed and curiously interleaving and offsetting the horizontal concrete bands.

Turning the corner on Pratt Walk, with its row of elegant yet modest 18th-century terraces, stands a large concrete monolith: an elongated cross shape in profile with curves in the corners and half-lozenge cut-outs on the two arms. The side facing Lambeth Road is emblazoned with the building's street number (likely not original), but from the side the structure's real function as an air vent becomes apparent, indicating that the building on the surface is perhaps only part of a much larger complex.

Further down Pratt Walk, the building's entrance is tucked into a corner where it joins another, much larger structure that runs parallel to the adjacent rail line. This is Brutalism not unlike what one might expect to find in East Berlin. Even the concrete escape stairs – usually the place for a sculptural flourish – are all straight lines. Apparently, the building is a police control centre, but who knows what really goes on in there.

NO PARKING

Lambeth Towers

George Finch, 1970–74
80 Kennington Road, SE11 6NJ

Just up the road from George Finch's Cotton Gardens Estate (16) are his Lambeth Towers. Where at Cotton Gardens Finch conceived three distinct towers visible from the street and the skyline, here he created a more complex composition. Responding to the open corner site across the park from the Imperial War Museum, he designed three interlocking towers and an adjoining lower-rise block all arranged at an angle. Rising amid the cluster and giving a strong vertical accent is a thin concrete tower containing the lift shaft and escape stairs. As at Cotton Gardens, the towers are divided into a rectilinear arrangement of bays, some projecting and others recessing, which, combined with the white in-fill panels, creates a high degree of legibility with each maisonette identifiable from the ground. A cluster of mobile telephone masts sadly disrupts the clarity of the original stepped skyline.

On the ground level, Finch provided a range of communal facilities and amenities, again reminiscent of what he realised at Cotton Gardens. The original doctors' surgery and medical facilities have been converted into a maths school, while the old persons' luncheon club now houses a restaurant. Despite the loss of this important piece of social infrastructure, the complex is now open to all, with everyone able to enjoy the splayed arms of the original concrete structure while dining on Chinese barbecue.

Langham House Close

Stirling and Gowan, 1957–58
Langham House Close, TW10 7JE

Langham House Close – also known as the Ham Common Flats – has a claim to be not just the first Brutalist building in London but the first Brutalist building anywhere in the UK. (The Smithsons' Hunstanton School in Norfolk is earlier, but hard to reconcile as completely Brutalist.) The development was designed by the young partnership of James Stirling and James Gowan, who soon after would win global acclaim with their Neo-Constructivist Engineering Building at the University of Leicester. At Langham House Close, in contrast, they adopted a more Corbusian mode, strongly influenced by the French-Swiss architect's Maisons Jaoul, with its alternating bands of brick and rough concrete.

Working for a private client, and with a modest budget, Stirling and Gowan eschewed Corbusier's more overt mannerisms in favour of tight rectilinear compositions: a three-storey block of 18 flats and two smaller blocks of two storeys, each containing six flats. A key point of departure – materially and formally – was how to deal with the long, narrow site, on the edge of the garden of an 18th-century villa. And to be sure, there is more than a hint of the Georgian terrace in both the use of yellow brick and the careful ordering of the façades. Yet there are also moments of sculptural expression, particularly in the concrete communal stairs and bridges – which are all the more powerful because of the way they seem to stand apart from the overarching system.

Lillington Gardens Estate

Darbourne & Darke, 1964-72
57 Vauxhall Bridge Road, SW1V 2LF

The Ronan Point disaster, which saw the corner of a tower block collapse following a gas explosion in 1968, is usually seen in retrospect as signalling the move away from high-rise residential developments, but the Lillington Gardens Estate shows that it was already well underway nearly a decade before. The project was won in a competition by the partnership of John Darbourne and Geoffrey Darke, with a scheme that combined innovative approaches to internal planning, notably making major use of scissor plans and split sections, with an interest in the urban patterns of the surrounding city.

The overall plan of the estate creates a kind of perimeter along Vauxhall Bridge Road to the north, where the blocks are cleverly insulated from the traffic by a section of greenery, and Tachbrook Street to the south. Inside are carefully landscaped gardens – an enclave of quiet seclusion. But rather than acting as a barrier between estate and city, the configuration of the blocks feels open and porous, stepping back to follow the contours of the street and arranged with irregularly projecting bays and balconies, conjuring a sense of movement to what in other hands could easily become monotonous and monolithic.

Materially, the estate is of reddish-brown brick with concrete accents, a palette inspired in general by its setting and, in particular, by George Edmund Street's St James-the-Less, which the estate almost surrounds. Like that church, the estate has a roughness to its form and finishes, coupled with an overriding generosity in its contribution to the city.

Ministry of Justice Offices (formerly the Home Office)

Fitzroy Robinson & Partners with Basil Spence, 1972–76
102 Petty France, SW1H 9AJ

All buildings are symbolic, even abstract ones, with their form, scale and materials conveying particular ideas, impressions and associations about the building itself and its occupants. It is impossible to know what image the Home Office wanted to convey for itself when this building was being commissioned. But if it wanted to give the appearance of being overbearing, faceless and defensive, then it is hard to think of a building that does this better.

This great hulking mass of a building, which now houses the Ministry of Justice (after the Home Office moved into new premises on Marsham Street), stands on a large site between Petty France and St James's Park. From the long spine range along Petty France protrude three wings: two towards the park and the other, which could almost be seen as a tower, to the east. All the wings are treated similarly, stepping out at their base and at their tops. One might surmise the intention was to allow the building to be read from different distances in different ways: the lower storeys aimed at the pedestrian, with large windows sitting in concrete frames; and the upper storeys read at a distance, with large windows behind concrete striations, and a sloping roof stepping back behind. However, the result is to make the building feel clumsy and lumpen at every angle, especially from the park, where it appears a vast ponderous pile.

Minories Car Park

City of London Architects' Department, 1968–69
1 Shorter Street, E1 8LP

When the Welbeck Street car park in Marylebone was threatened with redevelopment in the mid-2010s, it attracted what at the time seemed a surprising amount of attention – unfortunately this did little to prevent its demolition in 2018. But the loss will not have been in vain if it brings attention to London's other Brutalist car parks, notably Minories Car Park.

It stands on an island site just across from the Tower of London, hard up against the railway line to the north, with roads originally on all other sides (the western part of the car park was replaced with an office building in the 1980s). Its overall form is relatively simple, comprising a rectangular box raised up on piers, with a lorry park at ground level enclosed in brown brick and three levels for cars above. Those upper levels are left open thanks to a system of precast frames, with the apertures elegantly rounded in the corners and chamfered at the bottom. The corners are a particular highlight, with two vertical edge pieces fused together with a narrow gap between, giving a real sense of lightness when viewed obliquely. The adjoining car ramps are treated quite differently, with board-marked concrete for the ramps and an enclosing wall neatly striated and pick-hammered.

As a building type, car parks are hard to love, and it never seemed likely that Welbeck Street would be saved. But if one can look beyond the typology, Minories Car Park is a structure of rare sophistication and detailing.

SHORTER
STREET E1
Tower Hill
Tower of London
Wilton's Music Hall
Shadwell

National Archives at Kew

John Cecil Clavering for the Property Services Agency, 1977
Bessant Drive, TW9 4DU

The relationship of particular architectural styles to particular building types is a recurring theme in the history of architecture. A building's type rarely determines its style, but some styles are especially suited to some building types, or rather, there are some building types that allow a style to be the fullest expression of itself. Brutalism and archives are a good example of this, exemplified in the National Archives building at Kew in south-west London.

By the late 1960s, the Public Record Office, as it was then called, was outgrowing its premises on Chancery Lane in central London, so a new building was planned to provide more space and ensure the records were kept in the optimum conditions. The first requirement was that it would be big, the second that it would be strong (all that archival material is very heavy) and the third that it be easy to regulate heat, light and humidity. The result was a vast building, square in plan with canted corners, raised up on massive piers, with two wide horizontal bands of glazing with a thin band of concrete between. This arrangement then flips for the three storeys above with wide concrete bands interspersed with a narrow strip of windows.

The result is fortress-like – deliberately so – an effect that a later adjoining building, added in the 1990s, attempts to soften. Recent refits have sought to make the complex more welcoming, ensuring it becomes somewhere that's not just a repository used by researchers, but a cultural destination.

he Estate ur
National Theatre

National Theatre

Denys Lasdun & Partners, 1969–77
South Bank, SE1 9PX

'A clever way of building a nuclear power station in the middle of London' was how then Prince Charles once described the National Theatre. It is hard to think of a more wrong-headed assessment of any building, let alone one of the great buildings of post-war London.

The story of how the National Theatre came to be sited on London's South Bank and designed by Denys Lasdun is a long one involving sites in Bloomsbury and Kensington and several designs, including one by Edwin Lutyens. At first glance (and probably second and third glance too), Lasdun's design could not be more different from the conventional idea of what a theatre – national or otherwise – might look like. Rather than hidden away, the fly towers (which allow sets to be lifted above the stage) of its two main theatres – the Olivier and the Lyttelton – dominate its skyline. But in contrast to the singular sculptural form of Hans Scharoun's Berlin Philharmonie – its most obvious precedent – Lasdun created an almost geological composition of horizontal terraces layered on top of each other, all in raw board-marked concrete. Apparently, Lasdun's specifications were so exacting that the timber formwork could be used just three times before being replaced to ensure the prominence of the grain remained visible.

The result is a building full of geometrical vigour, but with little of the roughness one often associates with Brutalism, reflecting in a curious way something of the work of Lasdun's great hero, Nicholas Hawksmoor.

N

SLOW

Paddington British Rail Maintenance Depot

Paul Hamilton of Bicknell and Hamilton, 1966–68
West Block, 179 Harrow Road, W2 6NB

A triangular site hard up against a new elevated motorway is about as tricky as it gets for an architect, but the Paddington Maintenance Depot doesn't just manage to deal with this challenge, it almost makes a virtue of it. First off is the way its four levels sit so neatly on the partially sunken plot (excavated during construction of the motorway). Then there is the projection of its upper floors, which contain workshops and then offices above, and project over the ground-floor boiler rooms where the distinctive funnel-like chimneys emerge. There are entrances at two levels: ground floor and directly into the first floor from the adjoining roadway. The horizontality of the almost continuous ribbon windows and concrete bands between is balanced by the verticality of the stair and lift tower, with a curved and angular section that rises well above the roofline at the wider end of the building. There is a strong nautical feel to the composition, not just in the building's forms, but in the contrast between 'under' and 'above water': the former is all raw concrete, grey and rough, the latter is smooth, bright and streamlined – designed, it would seem, to be viewed at speed by cars from the elevated motorway.

Most Brutalism seems in its angularity to echo the starkness and abstract vigour of Russian Constructivism. But this building, with its smooth, sinewy forms, picks up the thread of interwar Expressionism to create a supremely elegant solution to a most unpromising site.

Perronet House

Roger Walters, 1969–70
44 Princess Street, SE1 6JR

Elephant and Castle was heavily bombed during the Blitz and became a key redevelopment site in the decades that followed. Around the two major roundabouts rose Ernő Goldfinger's Alexander Fleming House, the shopping centre – one of the first in the UK – by Boissevain & Osmond, the Corbusian Draper Estate to the south, the vast Heygate Estate to the east, a tower for the then London College of Printing, and Rodney Gordon's Faraday Memorial. Much of this redevelopment has now gone in a wave of 21st-century gentrification. One of the buildings that remains was one of the best: Perronet House.

It was designed by Roger Walters, then chief architect of the Greater London Council, who would also oversee the design of the Thames Barrier and the sensitive rejuvenation of Covent Garden market. By the late 1960s, the tide was turning against high-rises, and Walters was in any case interested in housing where the community could be integrated, rather than stratified. So here he conceived a scissor-section system, with flats split across three levels, and accessed via a half level, visible in the projecting windows on the end elevations. The whole composition was raised up on *pilotis* and a podium, so it stood away from the traffic (though this was largely filled in with additional flats in the 1990s). Although the material styling and finishes are towards the rougher end of Brutalism, it is a building that is full of humanity, a place of life and community.

20
Controlled
ZONE
Mon - Fri

Royal College of Art, Darwin Building

HT Cadbury-Brown with Hugh Casson and Robert Goodden, 1960-63
Kensington Gore, SW7 2EU

London is a city of contrasts but there are surely none more stark than between the bombastic High Victorian grandeur of the Royal Albert Hall and the dark, austere rectilinearity of the adjacent Royal College of Art building.

The principal requirement for the main teaching building was open and flexible interior spaces with the requisite strength to accommodate large pieces of heavy equipment and machinery. Cadbury-Brown's solution was a rectangular block of eight storeys, with projecting stair cores on the south and north sides (the latter includes a lift). The even numbered floors are split level, which is expressed in the contrasts between the side and end elevations where the rhythm of the façade becomes faster and more even. The top two floors are set back and presented as four projecting units.

Two smaller blocks join the composition to the south. Where the main Darwin Building is rigidly rectilinear, these, in contrast, are more angular to neatly fit within the tight site. Directly facing the Albert Hall is the Gulbenkian Wing, which contains gallery spaces, in low dark brick with a concrete cornice and columns either side of the entrance. Then, on Jay Mews, is an even more angled building with exposed concrete floor slabs containing offices, common rooms and other spaces ancillary to the main teaching spaces.

The result is almost factory-like in its austerity and raw surfaces – a synthesis of Modernist principles of art education and design – but rendered with finesse and elegance.

THE
ROYAL COLLEGE
OF PHYSICIANS

Royal College of Physicians

Denys Lasdun & Partners, 1960-64
11 St Andrews Place, NW1 4LE

Rising amid the stuccoed terraces and grand villas surrounding Regent's Park is somewhat surprisingly one of London's greatest Brutalist buildings. Lasdun's Royal College of Physicians is both stark in its abstract massing, yet elegant in form and manner, and the perfect foil to its Classical surroundings.

The building is T-shaped in plan: to the east is a horizontal wing of offices that complete the terrace on Albany Street; to the west, projecting from the offices, is a rectangular block containing all the principal ceremonial spaces. Approaching the block from Outer Circle, one is met by what at first glance is a familiarly Brutalist inverted ziggurat arrangement, but unusually here the projections are supported by a trio of central posts or columns: two skinny ones supporting the higher storey (which contains the library) and a thicker, sturdier one supporting the lower one. The arrangement gives the composition an overt, almost Classical symmetry, accentuated by the pairs of slit windows at the outer edges. This symmetry is brought into dynamic tension by the off-centre lift shaft that rises from the flat roof behind, which continues to the south elevation with the asymmetrically protruding box of the Censors' Room and the irregularly shaped lecture theatre of blue engineering brick.

The interior revolves around the central staircase hall, which gently winds its way up the full height of the building, with galleries running around the perimeter. Its lightness cleverly contrasts with the harder exterior.

29

Royal National Theatre Studio (formerly Old Vic Theatre Annexe)

Lyons, Israel and Ellis, 1957–58
The Cut, SE1 8LL

The architects Lyons, Israel and Ellis have a good claim to being called the godfathers of English Brutalism. Many key Brutalist architects would pass through their offices, among them James Stirling, James Gowan, Alan Colquhoun and Neave Brown, before leaving to chart their own course. Although now overshadowed by the work of those more famous figures, the practice was nevertheless itself one of Brutalism's leading exponents during the 1950s and 1960s. Among its most striking works from the period was the Old Vic Theatre Annexe, now the Royal National Theatre Studio.

Theatre workshops are an unusual building type, and these have the distinction of being the only architect-designed examples ever to be built in Britain. The project arose as a result of the Old Vic theatre becoming the first home of the National Theatre Company (which would later move to Lasdun's riverside building (36)) and the need for facilities for scenery painting and construction, wardrobe and offices. The architectural response was a building with exposed concrete frame and brick infill which quietly yet confidently occupies its corner site.

The building is arranged in two halves: the first, facing The Cut, contains glazed offices at ground level, with workshops above. The rear is a double-height space for scenery painting. Overall, the composition is robust, almost functionalist with its expressed sloping roof and lift tower, but not without a sculptural flair, particularly in the glazed escape stair to the east.

Salters' Hall

Basil Spence, Bonnington & Collins, John S Bonnington Partnership, 1972–76
4 Fore Street, EC2Y 5DE

One of the great pleasures of walking around the City of London is the often extreme architectural juxtapositions and the way buildings suddenly appear as if out of nowhere. This is no more the case than with the Salters' Hall – a building of brilliant crystalline white concrete surrounded by the ubiquitous steel and glass, and the dark brown of the adjacent Barbican.

The Salters are one of the City's livery companies, essentially guilds that go back to the Middle Ages. The previous Salters' Hall was destroyed in the Blitz and a competition was held to design its replacement, which was won by Basil Spence, who would go on to realise what is actually the Salters' seventh hall. Spence conceived a vigorous composition of interlocking horizontal and vertical forms. The lower levels, which contain offices, are relatively heavily glazed, while the top three floors, which accommodate the Salters' Company itself, have more of a balance between concrete and glass, with the composition shaped by an almost functionalist relation to the configuration of interior spaces.

The interiors themselves were realised in collaboration with the interior designer, David Nightingale Hicks. The lobby to the hall has gentle allusions to a salt cave, while the hall itself is a stunning double-height space lined in ash. This is Brutalism at its most refined, a building with the craft and attention to detail of a finely worked piece of furniture.

SOAS

SOAS Library

Denys Lasdun & Partners, 1970–74
Thornhaugh Street, WC1H 0XG

The School of Oriental and African Studies moved from its original location on Finsbury Circus before the war into a building designed by Charles Holden. Plans for further buildings went unrealised. Thus, like Lasdun's adjacent Institute of Education building (26), the library that he would eventually realise for SOAS in the 1970s, derived ultimately from Leslie Martin and Trevor Dannatt's 1959 University of London masterplan.

Although Lasdun was appointed as early as 1960, planning approval was only granted in 1968, by which time Lasdun was able to significantly depart from Martin and Dannatt's masterplan. Instead of repeating the Institute of Education's long spine block, which would have necessitated the demolition of the whole western range of Woburn Square, Lasdun conceived a square pavilion adjoining Holden's existing building, through which it is entered. Externally, the building contrasts significantly with the adjacent Institute of Education, having a tonal uniformity between glazing and concrete, and rising vertically with horizontally oriented façades split into nine bays with circulation cores protruding above the flat roof. The interior revolves around the central atrium, which is faced by three levels of balconies lined with flat concrete panels and oversailed by a glazed ceiling with concrete beams intersecting diagonally.

Modest changes in the 1990s by John McAslan & Partners, including the glazing in of previously external terraces, apparently had Lasdun's approval.

HAYWARD
NARA

Southbank Centre: Queen Elizabeth Hall, Purcell Room and Hayward Gallery

London County Council Architects' Department (chief architect Hubert Bennett), 1963–68
South Bank, SE1 8XX

Just a decade and a half separates the opening of the Southbank Centre and the Royal Festival Hall, but architecturally they are much further apart. In contrast to the Festival Hall's polite Scandinavian Modernism, the Southbank Centre is a disordered assemblage of connected forms and volumes. Materially, the Festival Hall's polished surfaces and rarefied materials give way, at the Southbank Centre, to a rough and abrasive mixture of cast-in-place and precast concrete panels. If the Festival Hall represents cultural continuum, then the Southbank Centre is about rupture.

The startling arrangement of forms derives in part from three distinct requirements: gallery, concert hall and smaller recital room. The latter two are relatively conventional in their interior arrangements, but the Hayward Gallery is something else: a complex configuration of different spaces across multiple levels with the raw concrete a constant – and some say distracting – presence.

From the beginning, the building was conceived as somewhere that would help facilitate new forms of culture, with the exterior decks intended to provide platforms for spontaneous activity. With the exception of the skateboarders in the undercroft, it never quite worked out that way, with the failure often put down to the weather (something that Richard Rogers once planned to alleviate with a huge glass roof). Yet, this bloody-minded disregard for comfort and practicality is actually what gives the building its energy.

BANK
RE
beth Hall
Room

Southwyck House

Lambeth Architects' Department, led by Magda Borowiecka, 1972–81
Coldharbour Lane, SW9

In 1969, the Greater London Council published a traffic plan that proposed encircling inner London with a six-lane urban motorway, known as Ringway 1. Brixton was designated to be the site of a major interchange with a further motorway heading south. If built, this would have laid waste to vast swathes of central Brixton, which would have re-emerged as a mass of towers, slab blocks and megastructures. Fortunately, the proposal was dropped a few years later, but in Southwyck House there stands a relic of a future that never was.

Running along Coldharbour Lane, parallel to the train line, Southwyck House is a 250-metre-long composition of four nine-storey-tall slab blocks and two further blocks stepping down at the side. It is known locally as the 'Barrier Block' and for good reason, with the frontage facing Coldharbour Lane acting as a vast wall articulated by tiny windows, with thick concrete bands rising and falling, and the concrete stair towers between each block.

While it looks strange today, the composition makes sense given that the elevated urban motorway was planned to run directly adjacent to it, with the building conceived to act as an acoustic shield for the estate behind. As architect Magda Borowiecka recalled, 'The motorway would have been 60 feet up in the air, so I needed to create a blank wall going up higher than that. It was rather miserable and I had to think of some way to make an interesting building.' Something she certainly achieved in composing one of London's most imposing Brutalist landmarks.

St GILES HOTEL
ST GILES CASINO
CASINO
SLOTS LOUNGE
Mon - Sat
9 am - 7 pm
OLE & STEEN
ping pong
20

St Giles Hotel

Elsworth Sykes Partnership, 1971–77
Bedford Avenue, WC1B 3GH

For such a large and uncompromising building, the St Giles Hotel is relatively little known. Sited where Great Russell Street and Bedford Avenue meet Tottenham Court Road, it stands literally and metaphorically in the shadow of the nearby Centre Point (13). The building is composed in two distinct levels. A two-storey podium fills the irregularly shaped plot, the floors articulated by a hefty band of textured concrete continuous to the front and rear, but articulated on the side elevations by heavy faceted precast concrete piers. These piers visually connect to the level above: four slabs that extend the full width of the plot. Moving from west to east, their heights rise and then fall quickly in a way that is far from contextual, though does at least acknowledge their surroundings. The ends of each of the four blocks project over the side of the plinth supported by a giant stepped bracket. In plan they are more or less identical: elongated diamonds with the point ends sawn off parallel with the street frontage, oddly not unlike Centre Point. Here, the precast concrete panel construction is composed in such a way that the windows either look north or south, thereby maximising the number of rooms that can be contained on the site.

The result is a building that, depending on where it is seen, is at times dark and heavy – presenting a blank, closed-off face to its surroundings – but at others open, layered and dynamic.

Standard Hotel (formerly Camden Town Hall Annexe)

Camden Architects' Department, 1977
Argyle Street, WC1H 8EG

Recent years have seen a number of examples of redundant Brutalist buildings being imaginatively retrofitted and brought back into use. Increasingly, these retrofits don't try to soften a building's Brutalist qualities but lean into them and embrace their 1970s feel.

One of the best examples is the Standard Hotel on London's Euston Road, directly across from George Gilbert Scott's Neo-Gothic Grade I-listed Midland Grand Hotel. It was built by Camden Council's celebrated architects' department as an annexe to the Classical Camden Town Hall next door. As a result of the regeneration of the King's Cross area in the 2010s, and faced with significant bills for repair, Camden sold the building in 2014. The buyers were the Standard, a small international chain of high-end boutique hotels with a reputation for the risqué that perfectly matched the building's Brutalist edginess.

Under the direction of Orms Architects, the building's egg-box-like precast concrete façades were cleaned up and a new three-storey extension added to the roof, its modular curved-corner forms echoing the original building below. A red bubble lift rises in a recession between the four equally sized bays to the west and the wider one to the east. The interiors, designed by Shawn Hausman, the Standard's in-house designer, and the interior architects Archer Humphryes, are a riotous pastiche of 1970s design with references to everything from *Logan's Run* to the London Underground.

Stoke Newington School

Stillman and Eastwick-Field, 1967–70
Clissold Road, N16 9EX

The three university friends John Stillman and John and Elizabeth Eastwick-Field set up their practice in an office on Dean Street in Soho in 1949, and soon began to develop a reputation for their calm, well-ordered designs. Schools became a particular speciality, with the practice completing projects in London, Cheshire, Devon and later Gibraltar – underpinned by the belief that light, airy, well-detailed and functional modern buildings could help improve educational outcomes.

The practice's Clissold School, now Stoke Newington School, exemplifies this approach. It comprises a rectilinear grouping of three-storey, flat-roofed buildings arranged around courtyards of different sizes and degrees of openness. The material palette is reduced to brick and concrete, with both used in ways that are forceful yet restrained. Concrete bands extend from the floor slabs to articulate the flat expanse of brick. The glazing continues the abstract language but in a similarly understated manner, with typically careful detailing. The only hints of flourish are the projecting glazed pavilion to the south, a glazed stair on one of the blocks to the north and the concrete escape stairs.

The boilerhouse at the northernmost edge of the complex is both a departure from the composition and a continuation of its design language: an angled roof, rough concrete skeletal frame and the machinery visible through the wide glazing. This is Brutalism as a backdrop to everyday life.

Strand Building; Macadam Building, King's College

Troup, Steele & Scott, 1966–71; 1972–75
Surrey Street, WC2R 2NS

King's College was founded in 1829 and allocated land to the east of Somerset House, where it quickly erected a building by Robert Smirke, in keeping with the Neoclassical masterwork by William Chambers. But the new university was unable to acquire land to the north, so its Strand frontage was limited to a very modest gateway – which the present building finally rectified.

The façade is split into horizontal sections: the first is defined by the piers and heavy floor slab; these are then overhung by four further storeys with a boldly protruding precast concrete frame; T-shaped elements are inserted as a screen to the windows behind. This is then topped by two further storeys, which are treated completely differently: they are set back with windows running the full length and smooth concrete bands between.

It was originally intended that the Strand building would run down Surrey Street and connect to a building facing the Thames. In the end, it was only the latter that was built, with the two Brutalist edifices serving to bookend the otherwise Neoclassical site. The Thames building continues the same language as the Strand building, omitting the top section, but gaining a lower one in the form of a relatively plain brick building with vertical windows that accounts for the significant drop in ground levels. Although a little ungainly, it provides a much better complement to Somerset House's regal Neoclassicism than the brick buildings adjacent to it.

SULKIN HOUSE
NOTICE

Sulkin House; Trevelyan House

Denys Lasdun of Fry, Drew, Drake and Lasdun (Margaret Rodd assistant architect), 1955-58
Morpeth Street; Knottisford Street, E2 0RS

Critics of post-war housing often try to reduce it to either point or slab blocks. And, for sure, there were a lot of both constructed, but as these two identical blocks by Lasdun illustrate, this critique ignores the extraordinary typological and formal innovation that this period did not just allowed, but actively encouraged – and from early on. This isn't exclusive to the work of public sector architects. We can see it in private practices brought in to design council housing, which was how the young Lasdun – working in partnership with Maxwell Fry, Jane Drew and Lindsay Drake – ended up designing several projects in Bethnal Green.

The immediate context of nearby 1940s housing – functional but limited in ambition – reveals how much of a departure Lasdun's design was for the site at the time. The two identical blocks are what is known as 'cluster blocks', that is, wing-shaped in plan with a central service and stair tower. The intention was to create a high-density but more compact block than a tower or slab, while offering more opportunities for social interaction. Also critical was that residents could identify their flats from the ground, so each dwelling was clearly articulated in the fenestration, balconies and brick infill.

The two blocks pre-empt ideas that Lasdun would develop on a larger and more complex scale at the nearby Keeling House (27). Where that building pre-empts 1960s Brutalism, these are more obviously 1950s – more modest in massing and materials, but arguably more radical in their departure from the norm.

Thamesmead

Greater London Council Architects' Department, led by Robert Rigg, 1967-69
Coralline Walk, SE2

Thamesmead is the most ambitious single development of post-war London. Built on the edge of the city, on marshland and the site of a former munitions factory, it followed the orthodoxy that underpinned post-war planning of moving populations from city centres to suburban locations. As originally conceived by the Greater London Council's architects' department, led by divisional architect Robert Rigg, it was intended to provide accommodation for 60,000 residents. The risk of flooding was a major concern during the planning process, so the development was arranged around several lakes (Southmere being the largest) that could accommodate run-off in the event of major downpours or inundation. In the original design, flats were also raised up on the first floor or higher, with the ground floors left for garages.

The estate featured a range of typologies by now familiar to Brutalist housing: long spine blocks that stepped back to create balconies and ensure good light for all levels, lower-rise blocks arranged into interleaved courtyards, and the estate's most distinctive feature: the 12-storey point blocks in rough grey concrete, their height apparently limited by pollution from a nearby industry.

Early photographs capture a strangely futuristic urban landscape of angular concrete forms and elevated platforms and walkways rising from expanses of water. It was no surprise that the estate would attract filmmakers, most notably Stanley Kubrick in *A Clockwork Orange*.

Supermarket
store
PRIVATE PARKING
RESIDENTS ONLY

Drury Lane Dental Care
Incorporating Preventive Dental Care Practice
59
Travelodge
Accessible Entrance

Travelodge Covent Garden

Geoffrey Spyer & Partners, 1972
10 Drury Lane, WC2B 5RE

One of the things that distinguished Brutalism from other forms of Modern architecture was its interest in the city 'as found', rather than as something to be rebuilt from scratch. Nevertheless, it still often reflected the antagonism to the street as the fundamental urban unit that had driven the first generation of the Modern Movement. This is perhaps why the hotel at the top end of Drury Lane acts to evade its position on one of London's historic thoroughfares.

Approaching the building from Drury Lane, it rises up as an arresting irregular mass of concrete forms. Up is the operative word here, because the composition stands on a plinth with access from the street provided by two angled sets of steps that lead to a partially enclosed courtyard overlooked on three sides by wings of different heights. This arrangement allows the maximum number of windows, and thereby rooms, to be squeezed into the site.

Common to all the four wings is a structural system of precast concrete panels that create a kind of alternating columnar arrangement with windows set back in chamfered-edged compartments. The system is rather more elegant than it looks at first glance, with clever detailing allowing windows to be positioned in the corners. The service towers, in contrast to the accommodation wings, are treated as solid forms with a rugged striated finish. The lowest is finished with a glazed canted corner that creates a neat contrast to the modular form of the accommodation block behind.

Trellick Tower

Ernő Goldfinger, 1968–72
Golborne Road, W10

Rising over the railway tracks leading out of Paddington Station, Trellick Tower looms like a phantom of a London that once was. It was commissioned by the Greater London Council in 1966 and completed six years later. Its design closely follows that of Goldfinger's slightly earlier Balfron Tower (5) in east London. Perhaps befitting its west London location, and following the lessons Goldfinger learned while living at Balfron for several months after its completion, Trellick feels more resolved. It is as confronting in its appearance and as polemical in its social programme and political underpinnings, but slightly more polished in form – especially the service tower – and in materials, with marble-lined halls and cedar balcony railings.

Like Balfron, it is composed as a wide accommodation tower with an adjacent service and vertical circulation tower attached by walkways at every third floor. Trellick, however, is taller, rising to 31 storeys and containing 217 flats and maisonettes, with the latter positioned at the 23rd and 24th floors – higher than at Balfron – visible as a break in the otherwise consistently repeating floor elevations.

The idea that the building might play an active role in fostering opportunities for social interaction among residents is, again like Balfron, at the heart of Goldfinger's design. This extends to the adjoining seven-storey block and other lower-rise blocks that complement the tower, containing further housing alongside shops and a youth centre.

TRELLIC
TREL

TOWER

UNIVERSITY OF WESTMINSTER
OPEN DAY
#WEAREWESTMINSTER
UNIVERSITY OF WESTMINSTER
UNDERGRADUATE OPEN DAY SATURDAY
IT ALL STARTS HERE

University of Westminster

Lyons, Israel and Ellis, 1965–68
115 New Cavendish Street, W1W 6UW

The Robbins Report into UK higher education led to a major expansion of universities and heralded a new generation of polytechnics across the country, focusing on engineering, applied sciences and technical training. The Polytechnic of Central London, as the University of Westminster was then known, significantly pre-dated this, going back to 1838, but its major expansion as a federal body beginning in 1960 took place in tandem with this wider process.

New sites were identified for the College of Architecture and Advanced Building Technology on Marylebone Road, and the College of Engineering and Science on New Cavendish Street. Lyons, Israel and Ellis were awarded the latter commission due to their strong track record in education buildings, and perhaps also the fact that Frank Israel and Tom Ellis were alumni.

Lying almost immediately beneath the Post Office Tower, the site was a tricky one. The corner of Cleveland and New Cavendish Streets was the least hemmed in and was reserved for the boldest formal expression: a cranked seven-storey block to the north, with dark glazing contrasting against the white concrete service towers. Then, to the west, a longer, lower-rise block, continuing the same language, entered via a raised podium leading to a heroically cantilevered auditorium. There have been a number of alterations over the years, including the addition of a relatively sympathetic north wing. But the power and dynamism of the original composition remain intact.

15
LO69 UBP

Weeks Hall, Imperial College

Richard Sheppard & Partners, 1958–59
16–18 Prince's Gardens, SW7 1NE

Weeks Hall is all that survives of one of the great set-piece compositions combining old and new of 1960s London. On the southern side of Prince's Gardens in grand South Kensington stood a Unité d'Habitation-inspired block of student housing. It comprised stacked floors of student rooms, an elevated 'street in the sky', and cafés and communal spaces, available not just for residents but the entire student community.

Weeks Hall, which stands just off the north-east of Prince's Gardens, was in many ways the prototype for this scheme. Where Southside Halls – as it was somewhat unimaginatively named – was long and wide, Weeks Hall is tall and slender: a façade grid of four units rising ten storeys. The concrete frame is expressed between each of the units, which are broken down by the vertical and horizontal glazing bars, giving the composition a more dynamic quality than that expressed purely by the grid. On the side is a semicircular staircase that protrudes from the blank concrete facing almost like the apse of a Romanesque church.

One of the intentions behind Weeks Hall was to galvanise support for the eventual development of three sides of Prince's Gardens. In the end, it was only Southside that was developed, and with significant cost savings, though timber-lined interiors and spiral staircases were able to be retained. With refurbishment deemed impractical, Southside was demolished in 2005, leaving Weeks Hall a fragment of what might have been and what once was.

Weston Rise Estate

Howell, Killick, Partridge & Amis (HKPA), 1967–69
Penton Rise, WC1X

There is surely no more uncompromising building in London than HKPA's Weston Rise Estate. Built for the Greater London Council, it comprises five connected blocks that snake their way down the sloping site – their differing heights allowing for a consistent roofline.

The obvious precedent is the Park Hill Estate in Sheffield. However, tightly constrained on three sides, Weston Rise lacks Park Hill's geological elegance and the polychromatic brick façade treatment. What it gains is an arguably even more powerful expression of its concrete frame. Rather than the typically box-like arrangement with glass or brick infill, here the vertical elements read like columns with protruding flaps holding the aggregate-faced spandrel panels and lattice balcony frontages. The result is a composition that works at different scales: appearing almost like a textured weave from afar, but chunky up close.

Another interesting departure is the placement of the service towers that stand between and on the ends of the blocks, with their petal-shaped plans offsetting the rectilinearity of the accommodation blocks. The tower facing Weston Rise is treated differently from the others, with window boxes protruding from every other level with wonderful vigour.

Some of the concrete detailing has been painted to try to soften the overall effect. But if the building is fortress-like, as it is frequently described, it's worth thinking about what it is defending: the garden, playground and communal space that are sheltered by its kinked form.

One way

Whittington Estate

Camden Architects' Department (Peter Tábori and Ken Adie), 1972–79
30 Lulot Gardens, N19 5TR

During the 1960s and 1970s, the Camden architects' department was arguably the most progressive of any local authority, not just in London but in the whole UK. Under chief architect Sydney Cook, it pioneered new forms of high-density housing that, while avowedly Modern, drew from and reflected existing urban patterns, of which the Whittington Estate, also known as Highgate New Town, is a prime example.

It was designed by the Hungarian Peter Tábori, whose student diploma project Cook had spotted and was so enthralled by that he asked the young architect to work it up into the final design. The estate comprises 271 dwellings, housing 1,100 people, across six terraces arranged as half-ziggurats in a way that was becoming almost a signature for Camden projects, including, most dramatically, Neave Brown's Alexandra Road (02). The approach was especially suitable here because of the sloping site, ensuring all the homes get sunlight. The starkness of the stepped concrete forms is offset by the generous amount of space between each block and the timber-faced balconies, which allow for personalisation, often with plants. The interiors, designed by Tábori's architects' department colleague Ken Adie, were subdivided with panels and screens, permitting a large degree of flexibility.

Construction problems put the project well over budget, which contributed to later parts of the estate departing significantly from Tábori's Brutalist first phase.

P
PUBLIC CAR PARK
CONCEALED ENTRANCE

World's End Housing

HT Cadbury-Brown and Eric Lyons, 1969–75
Cremorne Road, SW10

The World's End Estate was one of the last large high-rise estates to be built in London, in part because of its long gestation in both design and construction. It was conceived by the Metropolitan Borough of Chelsea, which wanted to replace dilapidated Victorian terraces with a high-density estate. A design was commissioned from Eric Lyons, the architect famous for the low-rise housing estates he designed for the Span development company, which have now become classics of mid-century Modernist style. The ethos of his plan was to translate the qualities of his Span estates into a high-rise development.

After much wrangling, construction began in 1969, following Lyons's layout, but with the buildings significantly shaped by HT 'Jim' Cadbury-Brown, who had come together with Betty and John Metcalfe and Ivor Cunningham to help realise the project. The layout is an unusual figure of eight, with seven cluster blocks, each between 18 and 21 storeys tall, connected by lower blocks of nine storeys. All told, it comprises 750 dwellings, home to around 2,500 people.

The high-rise approach was to achieve the desired density, but also in response to the riverside location, with the seven blocks oriented to obtain the best views at sunset. Generous green space and various amenities are provided within the two rings. In their form, the blocks are as daring and as bold as any Brutalist housing in London of the era, but softened by the brown brick cladding of the concrete frame.

Index

Blue Crow Media
London, United Kingdom
bluecrowmedia.com

First published 2026

ISBN 978-1-912018-45-1

A CIP Catalogue record for this book
is available from the British Library.

Written by Owen Hopkins
Photographed by Nigel Green
Published by Derek Lamberton
Designed by Tuomi
Printed by Livonia Print

This book and other titles are available to purchase from bluecrowmedia.com.